E
Si81w

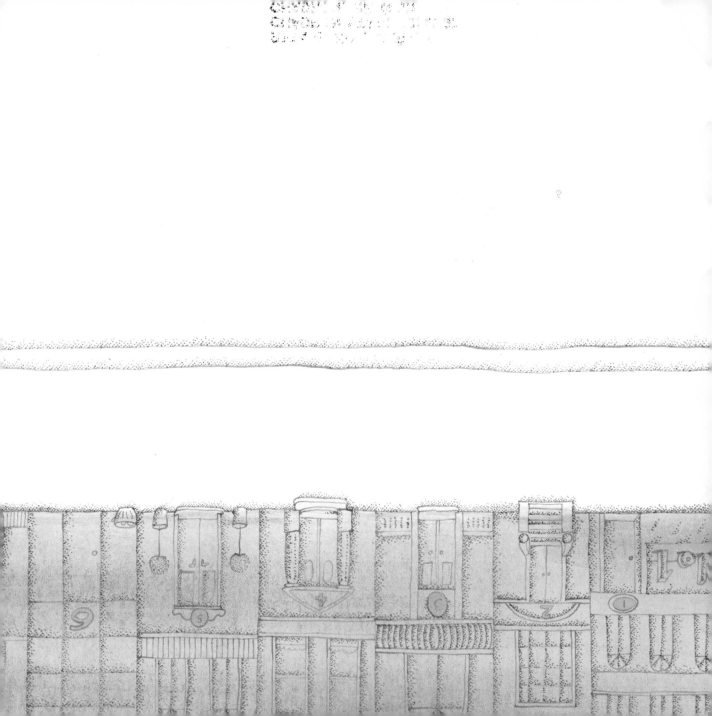

Waving

A COUNTING BOOK BY
PETER SIS

GREENWILLOW BOOKS

NEW YORK

FOR TERRI

Pen-and-ink and watercolors were used for the full-color art. The text type is Kabel Book.

Greenwillow Books, a division of William Morrow & Company, Inc., 105 Madison Avenue, New York, N.Y. 10016. Printed in Hong Kong by South China Printing Co. First Edition

10 9 8 7 6 5 4 3 2 1

Library of Congress Cataloging-in-Publication Data

Sis, Peter. Waving. Summary: As Mary and her mother walk down the street, they wave and are waved at by consecutively increasing numbers of people. [1. Walking—Fiction. 2. Counting] I. Title. PZ7.S6219Wav 1988 [E] 86-25762 ISBN 0-688-07159-7 ISBN 0-688-07160-0 (lib. bdg.)

1 taxi drove by.
Mary's mother waved for it.

2 bicyclists waved back at her.

3 boys walking dogs waved at the bicyclists.

4 girls in a car waved back at them.

5 mailmen
waved at the girls in the car.

6 police officers waved back at them.

7 waiters waved
at the police officers.

8 school children waved back at them.

9 Girl Scouts waved
at the school children.

10 joggers waved back at them.

11 musicians waved at the joggers.

12 tourists waved back at them.

13 Little Leaguers

waved at the tourists.

14 firemen waved back at them.

15 taxi drivers waved at everybody

waving at them.

And Mary
and her mother
walked home.

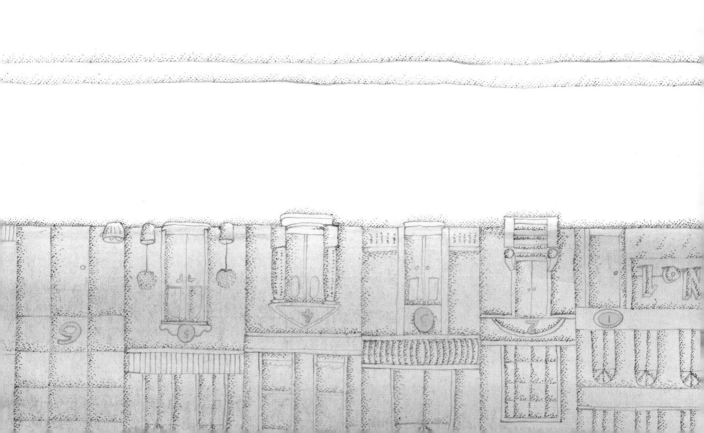